33.9 Million Miles From Lyme Regis

Laurie Avadis

This collection is copyright Cerasus Poetry © 2020

Individual poems remain copyright the author
Laurie Avadis © 2020

Cover design by Lee Playle
Scamp Factory Ltd
based on the author's photography

All rights reserved

No part of this book may be reproduced in any form or by any electronic or mechanical means, including information storage and retrieval systems, without permission in writing from the publisher, except by reviewers, who may quote brief passages in a review

ISBN: 9798625088039

Published by Cerasus Poetry
London N22 6LY

www.cerasuspoetry.com

To Mark Donnegan and Steve Lewis:
our shared laughter and music have changed my life
I could say I was grateful but it just would not be enough, my brothers

To Lee Playle:
it has been a long hard journey
but it has been all the better for having shared it with you

To Sam, Caroline and Walter Wilson:
your love has been unwavering and unquestioning
it is the greatest gift of my life

To Simone Bloom and Jackie Wilson:
no-one could have asked for better sisters
and your support has got me through

Foreword

Laurie Avadis is an interesting man. He's seen more than most, pushed his body further than most bodies get pushed and he's learnt along the way.

It takes someone special to then get all of that down on paper. This is undoubtedly a book of poetry but it's also a book of experience. It's no memoir, nor is it a biography. It's an expression of the lessons of his life and the emotions that have consumed him along the way.

We can all relate to the extremes of the human condition but we don't have to live them ourselves. Although one suspects that Laurie has lived through much of this, it is through the conduit of words – and for this poetry is an apt and able medium in the hands of a skilled practitioner – that we can learn of the joy and the suffering of our fellow man.

I've watched and read as Laurie's work developed over the past decade. It began as a primal scream and it has evolved into a complex but nevertheless accessible form in both prose and poetry. I've met the man from time to time and I must admit that I like him. He's always got something worthwhile to say, sociable, lively. He's keen to listen to others, he takes in his surroundings with care and he's open to new ideas at all times. This makes for that interesting man. Now, with the time and intelligence that it takes to develop his craft, he has produced a fine volume. These are poems that you will read over and over again and find something new with each approach. These are carefully chosen words from Laurie and we will all discover something about ourselves and the world in which we live from their reading. If you've got this far then read on. You are in for a treat!

Tony Cook,
Founder, ABCtales.com

Contents

On The Frayed Edge Of Functioning   1

The Emergency Bassoonist	2
The Whale Café	4
Her Father Was A Thunderstorm	5
She Had Not Aged Well	7
The Beekeeper Of Manhattan	9
The Pig Nest	11
One Direction	13
The Recipe For Making Bees	16

The Distant Thunder Of A Slammed Door   19

Where People Only Go To Work And From Which They Come Away Again At Night	20
Cannibal	22
I Am Running	24
Korn	25
Trampling Through Your Amygdala	27
Her Eyes Belonged To Infinity	28
My Name Is Destroy	30
Insert Coin And Squeeze	32
This Is A Place Of Moral Turpitude	35
The Business Of War	37
Of Rain And Of Shadow	38
Killing Little England	39
American Diaspora	40

I Am The Rabbit And You Are The Hat   43

I Am Your Imaginary Daughter   44
Rosalind   46
I Have Come Here For Your Name   47
Why Do You Fear Me   49
My Mother Was A Cyclops   50
You Are The Last Of Them   51
The Day Before The Day Before You Died   52
Dirty Little Footprints   54

She Will Be The Anthem For Your Heart   55

Atom By Atom   56
Love In A Time Of Riots   57
Everyone Remember Everything Eventually   58
Tiny Threats   60
I Knew She Was Corruptible   62
You Have Killed Our Fish   64
Her Eyes Became The Future   66
Other Trains   68
The Tear Collector   70
Her 64th Boyfriend   72
You WIll Not Age Well   74
Doubt Is My Mistress   75
Tangerine Static   77
The Duplicity Of Witches   79
On The Night When You Threw And I Ducked   80
Humbled By Darkness   81
War   82
Four Reasons To Fear Love   83
Mars   86

On The Frayed Edge Of Functioning

The Emergency Bassoonist

The emergency bassoonist
waits in his huddle-flat
on the frayed edge of functioning,
his telephone cradled
in his crumpled lap.
With each synchronous rotation
of his pursed purple lipped
lung cage,
the grapple hooks loosen.

The first few notes of
"Executioner Style" by
Kool G Rap
thrum-vibrate as he
flusters for the call
with twizzle fingers.
A smile dribble-leaks,
a fatal car jacking behind
Uno Mas?
in the heart of
Los Cabos,
an oboist and a violinist
gunned down,
a bassoonist
fatally wounded in the crossfire.

He gathers together
the offal of his
sanity,
like the remnants of Shelley's heart,
then places the instrument
into his quivering mouth
and blows with bronchial
effervescence,
bass and tenor clefs,
one treble, another.

Beginning to shiver,
he judder-squints
through
the contents
of his velveteen case.
Polish cloths, needle files,
low A extension, mini reeds,
a Glock 19,
10 rounds and one more
in the chamber.
He unfurls the city map
and shrugs on his
greatcoat,
to be wanted,
to be needed,
to be left,
to leave.

The Whale Café

This is the café in the park
where the whales come for breakfast
between the hours of 8 and 9.45am.
It is waitress service only and each whale has a favourite table.

Throughout the year, whatever the weather,
the gardeners sculpt and plant the sea bed
and sometimes
they sing in harmony with the mottled light
dancing on the skin
of the air bubbles
as they contort upwards
in perpetuity.

The whales are not big conversationalists.
They prefer to sit in
silence,
punctuated by the
rattle and hum of bone china
and the sea swoon swoosh,
as their giant tails
obfuscate far into
the silken vermillion.

This is a place for contemplation,
unchanged
for a hundred thousand generations.
It is a place of silent thunder,
where the vestigial fronds
of sentience are born.
It is a place we can never inhabit or own,
but if it dies,
we die.

Her Father Was A Thunderstorm

The years rained down on her
with the spite of playground punches.
She was brutalised by time,
the inhabitant
of an age
when those who aspired
towards the vector of truth floundered in a blinding shower of splinters,
when those who were jerked awake
yearned for the spectral anonymity of sleep,
when those who walked towards the light were slapped into darkness.

She had a sheepdog named Murder
and she lived in "Parthenon of Winter",
a commune
perched on a hilltop,
between Black Moss
and the Vale of Tears

On the bitterest of nights
and there were many,
she would take Murder out
to scour the moors for
stragglers,
until the golden green fragments of leaves
had sewn punctuation marks
in the snow around their feet.

Her father had been
a thunderstorm
you could hold in your hand,
a tsunami you could fold up
and keep in your pocket.
He told her she was immortal,
but he faded with the scars left
by betrayal,
leaving nothing more
than a beatific ache.

At night,
she would cling to Murder
so closely
that she could hear his
organs
reverberate.
His breath glowed
and she would watch it for hours,
circling the room
then settling
around her head,
to become
a spectral
crown of thorns.

She Had Not Aged Well

She had not aged well,
flora and fauna
grew within the rift valleys
below her eyes
and a legion of tiny ailerons
dragged the corners of her mouth
into a dystopian grimace.

This was the conspiracy of time,
its heft and yaw
smuggled into the cavities
deep within her skull
and the dreams,
the constant fucking dreams,
of hands and mouths
that belonged to those she had lost,
but never met.

Every morning
whilst she brushed her teeth,
she bleated a guttural mantra
to placate the universe.
It lacked the tonality of a prayer
and discomforted her husband
Larry,
who had recently secured a job
as the author of messages
for fortune cookies.

On Wednesdays,
she would leave her home
and make her way
to her local community college,
never certain
whether the rustle
in the bushes was the wind,
or the amorphous fingertips of death.

She painted tiny, intricate portraits
on the shells
of duck eggs,
each one so beautiful
it froze the breath
of her teacher
in his throat
and every week,
she wrapped a freshly painted egg
in a peppermint green and gold silk scarf
and crushed it to dust under the heel of her shoe.

Larry would have loved
those eggs,
he would have cradled them
in his palms
with the gentleness of a first kiss
and made a special place
on the mantelpiece
for each one,
beside the only photograph
they had
of their son.

But these were the verses
of the song of her loss
and the pain
was too exquisite
to share.

The Beekeeper Of Manhattan

It was 7.38am
when the beekeeper's right eyelid
shot open,
a parasol
snatched up into the maw
of a hurricane.

The eye consumed the interior
of the loft apartment
on the corner of Alphabet City's
Huston and 14th
and followed the late April sun
as it traced a sibilant slug trail of glistening mitochondria
across the discordant vinyl grooves
of Queen's "Sheer Heart Attack",
around the dark stuccoed lips
of the long deceased
Samoan doorman,
up the walls festooned with mould lilies,
to the oven baked orange
of the rusty nail head
that protruded from the
beekeeper's left wrist.

Seconds effervesced and
then decohered,
as the eye sashayed
around the outline
of the crucifix
where the beekeeper had been
nailed .

'Memo to self,'
thought the eye.
'I must be more careful
about who I borrow money from.'

'I need some air,' thought the eye,
drifting off into the biscuit haze.

It caught the
Staten Island Ferry,
before it took the Metro to the Hester Street Fair,
where it found the antiquarian book dealer,
as he basked in the aroma
of freshly baked churros and
Ecuadorian coffee -
not the shit you got on the Upper East Side,
but genuine Arabica Loja
from the foothills of Manabi.

The right hand
of the antiquarian book dealer
was a torpedo
from the blood black waters
of the Ligurian Sea
and the left hand
was a claw hammer
pockmarked by
a hundred thousand
tiny explosions.

The eye took a cab
to the northern end
of Grand Street
and left as the first metallic drops of rain
sent the shoppers chasséing for cover,
like 10,000 midget bullfighters.

It slid along the flaxen skeleton
of a sewer rat,
up to the loft apartment
and slid back into place,
just as the beekeeper's eyelids closed,
to hide from
the glare of another naked eternity.

The Pig Nest

There is a pig nest,
horse eye violet
and threaded with wool and steel,
in the upper branches
of the lurching night willow.

The pig nest is invisible;
neither squinting upwards
from the forest floor,
nor skimming the crepuscular sky,
offer even the
refraction
of its beguiling filigree.

Two by two piglet
eyes
grasp shrill glimpses of
the world
below.
On the shatter-ground,
a herd of tractors scatter from a water hole
at the sight of a skulking
lion ant.
Above:
a mosaic
of swooning pepper sun ferns
and positronic clouds.

Soon enough,
it will be time for the piglets
to leave their nest,
ushered by snout and tail.
Some will swirl on the breeze
with the bees and spitfires
and some will join the fall
without end.

Softly then,
stealing wool from the beards of thieves
and steel from the lair
of the buffalo wolves
in the upper branches
of the lurching night willow,
the pig nest begins again.

One Direction

When it was time,
she stepped out
on to
the window ledge,
her chip shop ultramarine
toe nails
pointed
to the face kiss concrete
ululating
beneath them.

> *A free fall occurs due to acceleration and hence its parameters of motion are independent of its mass.*

She wore a pink Terry nightie,
with a burn
on the right sleeve
you could
smell
but could not see.

> *Normally, the air resistance is very low, except in cases of objects with large surface areas and hence it is a safe bet to ignore that.*

Her
fringe
was dappled with
parsimony
and blew into her eyes
on days of heavy
fighting.

> *But at the same time one must realize that the force acquired by an object under free fall is certainly proportional to the mass of the object.*

The brutal, attenuated vision
of
the pedestrians of Lewisham,
glimpsed
between
articulated ankles,
ripped
the wrapping paper
behind her eyes
into jagged
strips.

In fact the force of the object is nothing but its net weight

'Things I like,'
she said to
a black faced gull,
its beak dipped in savagery
as it aquaplaned
on a
thermal
of curiosity,
inches
from her
face.

coupled with the net mass

'I like
red wine,
although the taste reminds me
of my music teacher's
endless,
porcelain fingers.'

of the object

'Tequila,
but it gives me heartburn.'

and also the momentum

'Absinthe,
although I can never
actually
recall
drinking it.'

of the object's mass

'Laughing as my first husband
slid off
the roof of our
semi detached,
three bedroomed
house
in Amersham.'

times the final velocity

'And the pure algebraic grace
of gravity,
of

$$F = G \frac{m_1 m_2}{r^2}$$

the ecstatic relief
that, at last,
I will be
travelling
in
only
one
direction.'

as it hits the ground.

The Recipe For Making Bees

It was almost 3.34am,
according to the watch face
tethered to his throat
by the c string
of a harpsichord,
intertwined
with the bitch green fronds
of a cypress.

He was a malingerer;
he malingered
outside Northwick Park station
and assailed commuters
with his
rapacious girth and earthy wit.

He wore an Alcatraz orange dress
sullied grey by predators
and when November
was at her most vengeful,
he would stand by the ticket machine,
fist his pucker-pink hands,
close his eyes
and hum a summer song
pitched beyond our grasp.

The commuters would stand and watch,
oblivious momentarily of the
war of terror and shame
and from his gelatine fingers,
the bees
would tremble,
tumble,
escape,
until he was
engulfed.

You could reach out
and stroke their
tiny beards
and
they would kiss lick pollen
behind your fingernails
and for as long as it took
for the honey to reach the back of your throat,
you could almost forget
you existed.

The Distant Thunder Of A Slammed Door

Where People Only Go To Work And From Which They Come Away Again At Night

He threw his newspaper
and seasick green rucksack
on to the station concourse,
grabbed the knot of my tie
and slapped me across the face
with an open palm.

Cromarty sea state slight or moderate, occasionally rough at first in the north.

My right eyebrow unzipped
and relieved itself,
an upturned ink pot
poured into my eye,
before his fist
tessellated my cheekbone into a jigsaw puzzle.

North Utsire cyclonic 4 or 5 decreasing 3 at times, moderate or good, visibility very poor.

My legs collapsed
and the glass ladder of reality
shattered,
as I clawed for rungs
that were no more than
stubs
and slid
and slipped.

Trafalgar wind Northerly 5 or 6, occasionally 7 later, becoming variable, 4 at times in far southeast.

'Fucking die, fucking die,'
sang his slavering skull mask,
as his right heel claw-hammered
metronomically,
conducting a symphony
of disfigurement,
until everything inside me
was as contorted
as the geology of my first lie.

Forties southwesterly force 8 to storm 10, occasionally violent storm 11, perhaps hurricane force 12 later in northwest.

The noise began after the storm ended,
with a fusillade of roaring
that became
so much a part of me,
you would think
it was impossible
for it ever
to be disentangled.

Sea State high becoming very high, occasionally phenomenal later in north, moderate or good.

It was a grand and tremulous sound,
the distant thunder of a
slammed door.

Cannibal

He said he was in rehab
and that his story
was an eloquent illustration
of the collateral damage
caused by
the wrong choice of parents.

He was the manager
of "Cannibal", a not-for-profit café
situated opposite
the halfway house in Shoreditch
where he had resided
(punctuated by sporadic relapses)
for the past three years.

'Don't act like you know me,'
he said, when I began to proffer
what passes for empathy
in the bloated mouths
of the Middle English.
His hands were as unsteady
as bomb shelters
on a battlefield
and he spilt much of my latté
into the saucer.

Our eyes entwined
in a tenuous waltz,
as we exchanged lives in that moment.
We were both slaves to addiction,
albeit different hues and increments;
we had strayed from the path
and found ourselves
beaten down, raw, attenuated.
Existence had become a muffled scream
at the beginning of each day,
never to be shared.

He looked at my latté
and dropped the cup
and half full saucer
down in front of me
with "fuck you" heavy-handedness.

He was a
recovering heroin addict
with a psychotic personality disorder
and a propensity
for acts of random violence.
We could have been brothers.

I Am Running

I am running,
I am to run.
I rip open my lungs on the bend by the last tree,
where the ground dips
into the bomb crater.
I dice with unfettered insanity as I pump arms
and scream like an angry child
towards the finishing line.
I scrape gored fingernails
in the pit I have excavated
in the rawest depths of my stomach
for the tiniest sliver of
more,
to reach that extra second
as the miles pile high and cruel upon my ruined chest.
I am agony and I am exultation;
my legs kick,
frenzied
with the death twitch of the gibbet.
I am blood
and I am ruin
and I am wrath,
my face is horror and my fibres detest me,
my feet strike the ground
as if blasphemed by the earth.
I am race end
and disintegration,
I am exultation
and sky scraping exuberance.
I am never again
and when next.
I am running,
I am untamed,
I am wilderness,
I am wildness,
I am to run.

Korn

In the week
that I was appointed
the deputy commissioning musical entertainment officer
for Ealing Technical College,
the commissioning entertainment officer was
killed
by a piano that fell
accidentally
out of the window
of the musical entertainment office.
Unlucky and ironic.
Thus, I was elevated
and with the annual Ealing Technical College Music Festival
only a month away,
it became my responsibility
to book the headline act.

I had intended to book Korn.
Korn are an American nu metal band from Bakersfield, California,
formed in 1993,
who have sold over 50 million albums worldwide.
Unfortunately, I booked Corn.
Corn are a Hungarian brother and sister duo who sing
medieval agrarian folk couplets,
backed by their father
Zsombor
on the harpsichord.
Corn have sold no albums worldwide.
The type of people who are interested in a concert headlined by
the popular American band Korn
are less likely to enjoy a concert headlined by Corn,
who are not popular in America
nor, it transpired,
are they even popular in the town of Pusztaszabolcs,
where they are based.
I discovered this on the morning of the "gig" when Zsombar,
who is 64 and clinically obese,
unloaded his harpsichord from the back of a camper van
and was very evidently not
a member of the popular American Nu metal band Korn.

A hurried telephone call to Korn's "people" provided
the unhappy news that Korn were not indeed free that evening
to play a gig at Ealing Technical College,
nor any evening,
in perpetuity.

So we persevered with Corn.

The mosh pit was cavernously empty.
The crowd surfing was limited to the harpsichord,
dragged from the stage
and dismantled with no little
dexterity.
The pogoing was unenthusiastic.
And before the end of the evening,
I had begun to scan the windows
above my head
for falling pianos.

Trampling Through Your Amygdala

Our friendship died today
in the front room
of your cottage,
murdered by moulting cats
and caravans
and buried amongst
stolen speakers

I knew you were weary,
beset by
the combined predation
of alcohol
and betrayal,
as their words slammed into you
day after day,
microscopic minotaurs
trampling through the maze of your amygdala,
until you collapsed.

You had been
away,
stultified,
hibernated, perpetual,
since we lost our voices,
but I never stopped hoping
I would hold you,
hold on to you
one last time
and inhale the
stubbled hegemony
of your stench,
that I might be transported
back
to the time
when were still
able
to drown out the static
and sleep.

Her Eyes Belonged To Infinity

'Don't fuck with me or I will hurt you.'
Her voice the grey green
of bruises
left by the rain on a forest floor,
she pressed the tip
of her home made shank
against
my trachea,
beside my oesophagus,
until butterfly kisses of blood
tattooed my collar.

I could grasp
only a snapshot of her face,
through the corner of my right eye;
it was cratered and indistinct,
as if it were a facet of the moon
glimpsed by a Victorian astronomer.

'I want...'
She corrected herself:
'I need you to give me all your money.'
Her voice was
etched with
first day at school
trepidation.

'I won't,' I whispered.

'I will fucking kill you then,'
she replied,
her breath
shallow, rapid;
her knife dug further
into my throat
until I could hear
my blood beg her to desist.

'

Then fucking kill me,' I replied.
'My life has been defined
by a series of threats
and yours is just one more.'

She hesitated,
then took a step backwards
and dropped the blade.
She was no more than 15,
but her eyes belonged
to infinity.
'You remind me of my father,'
she said.

My Name Is Destroy

My name is Destroy,
yet I am inert.
I was butchered
by an angel with wings
of blue pearl and honeydew
and now my body is inchoate.

'Get out of my space,'
the angel sang.
I was in the saloon bar of the
Hand and Two Sceptres
in East Dulwich
on a Saturday night
and I was wedged
between the contorted proboscises and antennae
as they thirsted, sucked and snorted
from endless flagons
of cellular gruel

'I am going to fuck you up,'
the angel told me.
As he set down his half supped pint,
his wings
coruscated in the firmament,
their gossamer tips brushed against the door
to the women's toilet.

I wove my fingers
into the shape
of a prayer
of supplication,
but his pursuit of vengeance was
indefatigable.

My body,
a million juddering spurs
of bone and spaghetti,
was crushed
against the
Star Wars themed fruit machine
with pernicious wrath.

'Help me,' I beseeched
the invertebrates.
'Redeem me,'
I begged the angel,
as my spine
made the sound
of the first breath
of a new born calf.

As I fell
on to the sick slick carpet,
as kick upon stamp
landed
and I felt the flesh of my
apotheosis
truly enter me,
I knew
that prayers and beer mats alike
lie abandoned
on the table tops
of smoke filled bars,
awaiting eternity.

Insert Coin And Squeeze

The girl with the cat boards the bus and sits opposite me.
Her lips form tumescent ellipses,
as her eyes fix mine
with hyperbolic ferocity.
'Are you staring at me?' she asks.
'No, I'm not,' I reply.
(I am staring at her.)
'Are you some sort of lonely pervert?' she asks.
'Can we break that question down into three parts?' I ask.
I glance at the cat.
'Don't ask me for advice,' it says.
'I am a dead end.'

'(a) I am not lonely,' I reply.
(I am so lonely that rats have burrowed down into my heart.)
'I am very popular - particularly amongst my contemporaries,' I add.
(She is the first person who has spoken to me in six months,
her voice is
the vibration of birdsong on the surface of the pools
that form in the mouths of
bougainvillea.)

'(b) You are of no interest to me.'
(I already love her a little.)

'And (c) I am not a pervert.'
(I have already envisioned our tryst:
she is a surprisingly gentle lover,
but I frighten her.
The marks left by my fingertips
on her forearms
resemble
the eastbound shuttle stops
of the San Francisco Ferry.)

She stands up,
her fists shoot from her pockets as if they are holsters,
the cat stares at the ceiling,
she has seen all of this before.
'Do you want it?' she asks.

There is face powder on the lapels of her blue jacket
and in it
there are tiny footprints
that spiral upwards towards her throat.
Her face is contorted,
a steel girder
with an unseen and fundamental flaw.
'Yes, I want it,' I reply.

The punches that rain down on me are nuptial kisses.
I have not been touched by a human being since
I was ushered out of a bus station
on New Year's Eve
for
praying to a poster
of David Beckham

Her fingers are in my hair now
and I reach out to touch her hands.
Her feelings for me are
vehement
and I have only gratitude.
I lie on the floor,
the underside
of her trainer
is on my face;
there is a brief hiatus
and I take the opportunity to watch a feature length film
about bee keeping
in my head.

Without warning, she helps me to my feet.
Her face is flushed,
she is barely eighteen and
already shrunken
by the weight of the anger
she carries.
She hands me the cat.
'You will need this,' she says
and gets off the bus.

The cat stares at me,
her breath is on my face.
'You are still alone,' she says.
The bus pulls away.

This Is A Place Of Moral Turpitude

I found a note
written in a florid style,
secreted in a rose bush
in a garden
situated
on the North Western edge of Cannons Park,
on the disputed border with Stanmore,
where the conflict
is at its most intense.

"Save me," it said and then,
in a different handwriting,
"Save me too."

The garden was bisected by a path
studded with
seashells
and beneath the swollen shadow
of a Magnolia tree,
under the wretched ochre and vermillion
of a shattered robin's egg,
I found a second note,
by yet another hand.

"You may have read the other note," it said.
"The provenance of its two authors is unknown.
I could never completely trust them and neither should you."

It began to rain,
tiny waterbound crotchets
dripped down the inside of my glasses
and into my beard.
As I turned to leave,
I slipped and suffered
a heavy fall.

My face nestled
against an angry rock
from which I saw,
nestled
within a sullen clump
of lavender
grown wooden
with neglect,
a third and last note.

"I bare no malice towards the authors of the first two notes,"
it read.
"They were abandoned here as you have been abandoned,
they fell here as you have fallen,
they must learn to accept
their place in the garden,
as must you"

And as the crimson whisper fell from my lips,
a duet with the rain falling around my ears,
a note was pinned to the cuff
of my greatcoat.

"P.S.
This is a place of moral turpitude."

The Business Of War

You asked me if I would like to go for a pint.
It was early December and your feet were already lying to you.
You had seen active service in Korea and your eyes drank cruelty
from the veins of thieves.
So many of your friends who had once defied gravity
and plunged towards the stars
with their mighty fists,
had become
no more than
crooked signposts
to the perfidious crepitus of time
in the grass behind
your local church,
to be cried and pissed on
in equal measure.

It was only a pint.
We would have shared our tales
of naked ambition,
of lusts and languors as vapid as Prospero,
as the landlord screamed 'time'
and Christmas Day bore down upon us,
the glittering whore
it has become.
But your invitation
stayed in my desk drawer
and the phone
remained in its cradle
and if I had asked you how that felt,
that tiny betrayal,
you would have told me
this
was the business of war.

Of Rain And Of Shadow

She wore red sequinned shoes
and every now and again, she
espied them
and part of her right eyelid
flickered.

When she sat down beside me
in the train carriage,
she laid siege to the armrest
and splayed
across into my leg space.

My fingers were forced to abandon my laptop to an uncertain fate
and retreat,
until I gave the impression
of a man in prayer.
I turned to the notebook on my mobile
and began to write.

Immediately, her face and upper body
became
as erect as a misericord.

'You writing about me in your fucking phone, you shabby little man?'
'Not you,' I said. 'No.'
'Why not?' she demanded. 'You could write the story of my life
in the time it will take to reach the next station.'
She was waiting for me to betray her,
as so many had,
as so many would.
She was made of shadow and I of rain
and neither of us were worth saving.

Killing Little England

We are legion,
but we are insects.
The bodies of our children return to us
from the killing fields
of Helmand Province,
intractable jigsaw puzzles
with missing pieces.

We are the benefactor and the begging bowl,
the mountain and the avalanche,
crouched in the dust of this perfidious Albion,
our fingers spiders' legs
that grasp for hegemony,
our averted eyes, insanity.

If every ragged word is true,
the ignominy of this rudderless, ruined boat
ships water with every new wave.
If our narcissistic governors
lead us not into temptation,
but to the very edge of the abyss and beyond,
are we too addled by the shisha pipe of celebrity,
blinded by the obolus that rest upon our eyes,
to fight back?

It is time (it is far beyond time)
to hunt them down until it is they
who cower in sewers,
to wrap their Etonian ties tightly
around their fat guzzle necks
and tell them,
this is our Grunwick, our Tulsa, our Bordeaux.
It ends here
and it ends now.

American Diaspora

On the drunken filigree
of midnight,
some time between
1987 and 1997,
(a decade I have disembowelled and entombed)
whilst one-shoe shuffling
beside
a fractured tenement promontory
in Lower East side Manhattan,
or the
defaced frontage
of the Ghurkha variety store
in Old Freak Street, Kathmandu,
I can't fucking remember
which,
I saw a flock of drug dealers
scooping the night up
into planished ultramarine eggshells
and downing it neat
with a shot of Yamasaki.

I crossed the road
into the path of
a cankerous behemoth,
dissembled
by a PCP Belushi speedball,
who
projectile slammed me
against the crocheted metallic shutters
of a dive bar.
Smash, smash, smash.

'Where have you hidden your spacecraft - give it to me,'
he crush-demanded,
my corneas dissattenuating
with every expulsive impact.
This was a difficult question
to answer.
'I swallowed it,' I replied.

'You can't hide it from me,'
he shrieked,
grabbing for my rib cage,
intent upon the
defenestration
of my internal organs.

Without warning,
to the melody of
a chainsaw
biting into sinew,
the drug dealers,
dimorphic, rapacious,
swarmed and expunged him,
leaving only his
gleaming white bones
for shark bait.

They turned to me,
their beaks heron-claw scarlet
and spoke
in a single voice.
'Will you join us?'
they asked,
their breath
fricative,
mingling with
their chameleon midnight bile,
sable wings softly
twitch-opening.

'You turn kings and queens
into electricity,
and live in a nest
weaved from stolen lies.
You are with many
but always alone,'
I told them.

'You keep the
shards
of your forever love
in a 5¢ Winstons tobacco
tin
under your pillow,'
they replied.
'For you,
hope has coalesced
into shallow perfidy;
for us, it is a commodity
we sell by the ounce.
Are we so very
different?'

I Am The Rabbit And You Are The Hat

I Am Your Imaginary Daughter

I have an imaginary daughter
whose age is as malleable
as the particulates of frost
freckled upon the eyelashes of
snowshoe hares.

'Don't stay out too late, Jezebel,'
I implore,
as she swish-sashays
down the staircase of our
Hollywood condo/ council flat/ houseboat.
'I worry about you just as much
as the parents of children who actually exist / were extant at some juncture.'
'I know daddy,' she says,
her eyes tingling with crepuscular grace.

'Your mother would have been so proud of you,' I say.
Grief clogs my amygdala
with the viscosity of dew dampened nuns.
'I wish I had known her,' Jezebel replies through kohl hued lips.
'Was she also imaginary?'
'Perhaps,' I answer.
'Always perhaps.'

'Do not ever leave me, Jezebel,' I say,
as I enfold her milkweed fingers
within my own.
'That is your choice, not mine daddy,' she replies.
'I am the rabbit and you
are the hat.'

'Will I marry?' asks Jezebel.
'Will I skip-fall in the playground?
Will I slam my bedroom door until the frame cracks?
Will I taste Milanese mozzarella?
Will I be tinged by hubris?
Will I curl up in a tartan chair in the big house?
Will I wallow in the shallows?'

'You will not,' I answer.

'Is this cruelty?' asks Jezebel.
'Are you cruel?'

'I am not,' I reply.

'What are you then?' she asks.

'I am your father,' I reply.

Rosalind

On the day that Rosalind died,
my sisters and I
stood in alignment,
3 celestial bodies in syzygy.

My brother-in-law
Brian
and I
carried the void she left in our lives
on our shoulders
to my airing cupboard,
where we hid it
in the snicket
between the bath towels
and the torn curtains
we do not have the heart
to throw away.

I felt blurred / slanted,
so he took me by the hand
and led me to the garden,
where dreams reside
in a state of temporal viscosity.

We fell on to our hands and knees
in the apricity
and searched for answers
hidden between newly laid robin's eggs
in the snow,
until our fingers and toes were red raw
and the clouds in the savage geometric prism
through which I see the world
had begun to clear.

I Have Come Here For Your Name

Her skin
was the colour
of the paper
teenagers use
for suicide notes.
She had a
half completed tattoo
of a red raw rose on her cheek,
a tendril of blood
snaked
down her face
and into the neckline
of her brutally white
shirt.

'This is my door,'
I said.
'Obviously,'
she replied.
'Why are you standing in front of
it?'
I asked.
'I have come here for your name,'
she said.

I dropped my car keys
into
the giant puddle
in my drive,
where the fox
was trapped
in the storm drain
and we watched
our reflected expressions
explode
and reform.

'Do you remember Linda,
the social worker you fucked
on the Trivial Pursuit board
in the flat you rented
above the McDonalds
in Golders Green?'
she asked.
'No,' I replied.
'She told me you were a cunt,'
she said.
'Oh yes,' I said. 'That Linda.'

Her eyes
(my eyes)
fixed upon the alien world
I occupied
with digital clarity;
she sculpted her mouth
into the shape
of a question mark
and stepped inside.

Why Do You Fear Me

This is the sketch you drew
of my father,
charcoal
on waste paper.

It was 1941:
you were 15,
wore
unmatched shoes
and lay screeching in the
bomb crater
where your family home in Shepherds Bush
had stood,
3 minutes before.

They sent you to the corner shop
to buy matzo meal, cabbage and
dill weed.
You would have taken your place
by their sides,
willingly,
as their eyes rose in unison
to greet perpetuity.

If you could carry on
after that,
if you could survive
with just a grocery bag
and a soundtrack
of the distant laughter of siblings,
who had been reduced to
cordite and verisimilitude,
then why did you fear your son so?

Are these his eyes -
replete of piety
and morality?
Is my smile as execrable?
Are my lips as thin and passionless?
Has my face become
our war?

My Mother Was A Cyclops

My mother was a cyclops:
she had the patina of humanity,
but hues of light and darkness
billowed and susurrated behind
her singular eye.

This did not make her easy to love.

My mother could touch the sky with her fingertips
and navigate between the architectural plasticity of her children's minds
as if she were an egret
and even when she was asleep,
her hands remained
a crystalline lattice
worn around our throats.

I lay with her
amongst her sun bleached bones
on the day before she died
and traced around her body
with a jagged stick of charcoal.

At first, she was the shape of a fish scream
washed ashore,
then she was the shape of my mouth
on the night my father fell
and the next day,
when she forgot how to breathe,
she became the shape of perpetuity.

You Are The Last Of Them

You are the last of them;
they have fallen,
no more than
tin ducks in a shooting gallery,
but you endure
in your tiny flat,
your confessional
walls banked by display cabinets,
their doors bulge to contain
a slurry of opaque memories.

The anecdotes you do not tell define you.
Time has you in its spiteful maw and you are
a rag doll
shaken,
stuffing pouring from multiple splits,
but you are stubborn,
you defy it.

Or perhaps it does not have the stomach for you.

We put you in your chariot
and swathed you and swaddled you in the rug my sister bought
and we walked the streets of Harrow,
streets you had not seen in years,
had not wanted to see again.

And when we sat together in a café to eat,
on that bitter winter's afternoon,
I could see at once that you were frozen to the bone,
but did not have the strength to tell me.
I went to you, held you in my arms and gave you my heat,
would have given you my blood.
I did not realize,
how could I have betrayed you to the cold?
But you had always expected me to.

The Day Before The Day Before You Died

The day before
the day before
you died,
I was the charismatic but ruthless leader
of a hundred thousand
Mogul warriors
as they battled
a rag-tag mercenary army
of astronauts, medieval knights and GIs
for supremacy over our
settee and coffee table.

You were not witness
to this senseless internecine carnage,
because you were at the office
where,
it latterly transpired,
you lived.

You were my almost father
and I was your nearly child.
You forgot how to smile,
while I was engaged in the business
of becoming dysfunctional.

On the evening before
the day before you died,
I returned home late
because three
meticulously cruel
classmates
had kicked me to the ground
and pelted me
with snow and stones
until I was hypothermic.
Such random acts
of attempted murder
were considered
to be
character-building,
in those days.

You were home
when I arrived
and led me wordlessly to the bathroom,
where you removed
my wretched, sodden clothes,
wrapped me in a towel
and put an uncertain
arm around me.

I was 11
and we had never had a single conversation.
You had fled across Europe
for 5 years
with the Nazis at your heels,
but your life
was never,
not for one moment,
more frightening
than in those few seconds,
when you realised
you had hidden
from the love
of your only son.

Dirty Little Footprints

Now it is winter,
the snow falls
and you can only walk
with the assistance of others.
You search for your tracks
but, as fast as you make them,
they are hidden.
We know what lies beneath, you and I,
when the hands that are claws
were boxing gloves
and the shoes that are useless weights
stamped and kicked.
There must have been school bound kisses,
the language of love cannot always have sat
as heavy as stones in your mouth,
even though you kept in,
locked away
and hidden,
there must have been
regret.

I have put away my Parka
and my shovel;
winter cannot erase, cannot exculpate
and I must not dig any deeper,
for fear of where the footprints
might lead.

She Will Be The Anthem For Your Heart

Atom By Atom

She has the kind of
immutable,
throat burstingly cruel
beauty
that makes men's eyes bleed
and women strafe their faces
with their
claws.

You need a shot
of pure hypoxic helium nitrate
to speak to her
and when her eyes
fall upon yours,
it is as if you are being
disseminated,
atom by atom,
febrile as the mist
rising from a
battlefield.

She does not have a name,
it is not necessary.
She resides in your
synapses and ventricles
and on the day you die,
she will be
the anthem
for your
heart.

Love In A Time Of Riots

I met you outside a ransacked Footlocker;
your fingers touched mine,
entwined.

As we pushed a Tesco's trolley
through the window,
shards of broken glass fell upon your shoulders
and into your hoodie,
glistening amethysts
flecked in their reflected hearts
with the blood orange glint
of burning shops and perfect hatred.

I bent down
and offered you
a single perfect red trainer.
We were alone on the planet in that moment,
our faces obscure behind football scarves,
but our singular purpose screamed eloquently
from our eyes:
destruction, obtuse and divine.

If I had never known a love,
or known what a life with love can be,
I knew it then,
as we were tasered
and dragged away together by our hair
and smashed
by special constables
and smashed.

Our landscape is empty and we share it with bitterness,
but the strength of the convictions you have given us
has led us to demonstrate how powerful
and how singular
this love we have for each other
is
and how much
we detest
you all.

Everyone Remembers Everything Eventually

Our first encounter
was as moon slugs
who slavered through the glass tilth of the regolith,
confined to parallel trajectories,
the earth sun baking
the black bow ties around our tiny necks,
dirt and pretty.

Then we were a pair of tears,
tracer ammunition
on the fustered cheeks
of a nightclub nubile
emerged from her cocoon
after a summer of estivation,
lusting yet lack lustre,
in the gaps between
the pounding beats.

I was an electron microscope
and you were a rare tropical virus
flattened between
smooth glass cheeks.
You squirmed dangerously,
flaunting your fascinator
under my
highest setting,
swelling so softly.

On a bastard bleached ochre beach,
we were North American desert tortoises.
You gave me a genuflective stare,
which added
silence to distance.
We drank,
our sides barely touching,
until we were betrayed
by time.

And now,
in this particular
gentle forever,
where we have neither danced
nor hidden,
you have sent me complicated Italian music,
photographs of tiny bridges
and asked me how it is
we have never met before.

And all I ask of you
is to remember.

Tiny Threats

Do you remember the day I forgot my shoes
and went to work in the rain?
I did not notice, because I had become
numb,
inured to the tiny threats
that lay upon my shoulders
and weighed me down.

I wandered into Starbucks
in Oxford Street,
my socked feet left a slug's trail
for those who shared my sodden path
to follow.

Having purchased an egg mayonnaise wrap,
I became dizzy
again
and I thought,
I do not want to die in here
amongst the half empty coffee cups
and decaffeinated choristers.

So I made it home,
as I would do
again and again,
as I did
until it was time to end my part
in this wretched war.

My feet were always wet
and yet
you never tired
of drying them
between your fingers.
You brushed the tiny threats
from my shoulders
and found new places
for me to hide
but,
when armistice was in sight,
you left
forever.

This is not a thank you,
although I have said that
so many times,
with fingers dug lifetime hard
into by palms.

Call it
a surrender.

I Knew She Was Corruptible

Her hair
had the property of maize
before
the males flower
and begin to shed pollen.

I watched
her index finger
as she
drew
a convex tetrahedron
in the dextrose
she had spilt
on the wretched palate
of her desktop.

I knew she was corruptible,
but
I didn't know
how.

After she had gone home
that evening,
I sat in her
leatherette
office chair,
smelt her
candy floss and nicotine
and saw
two
droplet chords
of blood
in the hinterland
of her
oversized
blotter.

I leant down
and touched them
with my tongue.
One tasted of poison,
the other of rapture.

It was after winter evensong,
the streets were muffle white
and empty.
I lay face down
in the snow
and begged for it to end.

You Have Killed Our Fish

They were snatched from their mother's teats
in the billow folds of the Ganges,
the supine lipids of the Bosporus
and more specifically
from The Surrey Aquatics Pet Megastore,
trapped by the duplicitous net
of the man with the ferocious contact dermatitis
and shepherded into a clear plastic bag
and from there to a shining
tower
of crystalline grandeur,
in the kitchen,
beside the scary coffee machine.

As they journeyed, they sang in unison,
'This is our salvation - our Euphrates -
we are the very few, the lucky few.'

Your hands are the gods of their hasty kingdom,
they supplicate them
with imperceptible prayers
and genuflect their gentle fins upon their Martian flesh.
They feed and scour and lift
the corpses of their brethren
up into the sky
and in
to bliss
and the green topped bin.

But lately,
your ardour for their shiny souls has waned,
they are to be consumed by your betrayal,
you have deflected their thin lipped platitudes,
crushed their sun in your palm,
stolen the teal petals
of air
with which they gilded their lair
and plunged them in to beer brown stillness.

'Save them,'
I beseech you.
'It's half past four in the morning,'
you reply.
'Save them,' I rejoin.
'Theirs will be an ignominious death,
deprived of sustenance and
of hope.'

You turn to me, your vulpine grimace pixelated by the light
of the digital
alarm clock.
'If it matters to you that much, you can fucking well clean the tank,'
you snarl.

But I am weak
and lumpen,
you
are a deity
and with your
mighty Marigold gloved hand,
you alone
can bestow beatitude,
or this
will be
their epitaph.

Her Eyes Became The Future

She was 6ft 7 and did not know what to do with it.
When we lay in the bathtub together in her apartment,
on afternoons when the bar work was slow,
her ankles projected
beyond my ears and
into the middle distance
with longitudinal exuberance.

This was the 1980s,
a time before emotions
had been invented.
Back then,
our relationship was
no more
than a cinnamon dusted chrysalis.

We would sit on the steps
of her brownstone
and watch the
pavement rabbits as they
scattered for cover in the snow,
their footprints
a mosaic semaphore for us to decipher.
She used a silver pipette
to drop question marks
into my mouth,
which pixilated and faded
like fireflies trapped in a spring downpour,
just beyond the periphery
of my vision.

On the nights
when the firestorms were
at their most intense
and the girders were smelted
into milky glass,
we smoked Ethiopian Highland
she grew from
Royal Queen seeds
and her eyes became the future.

'One day I will smash our love
until it is so many wicked shards,'
she told me.
'You will grasp them
to your chest
and try to make them whole,
but the pieces will slice you,
leaving ruinous scars
that never heal.'

We were propinquitas;
she drilled a mineshaft
into the side of my skull
and illuminated it with
Celine, Bonnard and Mingus.
I knew she would destroy me,
but in love and war
there are always
casualties.

Other Trains

Her voice ululated
amongst the Siberian air masses
caressing
the eastern slopes of the Urals.

For now,
she worked the tables
of a bar
clinging to the remnants of
the dockside:
a building
fashioned from the
hollowed out
exoskeleton
of a giant beetle,
but nevertheless benefitting from excellent
toilet facilities.

On my way to Kyiv
to give a lecture in deforestation
and entomology,
I had taken a 260 kilometre detour
to see Fleshgore, who play
Ukrainian death metal
and to collect mummified hind wings
from the carcasses of gigantic alien insects,
found below the surface of the Northern Polish wastelands.
It was that kind of trip.

'You should order the Draniki,'
she told me, as she took my hands
in the walk in larder
built within the insect's thorax.

We had met
just seconds before;
it was as if we were maquettes,
our every movement
predestined by puppeteers.

The locals call me "paskudnyak" - the scoundrel - she told me.
When I asked her why,
she writhed her attenuated fingers
around my wrists.
'This is not a normal landscape,'
she said.

'I am surrounded
by forests without trees,
colour trails in
an agate sky,
bisected by the parabola of chariots
and bile,'
I replied
and pulled free whilst I still could.

'This will be the happiest and the saddest day of your life,'
she whispered.

When I told her I had to leave
to catch my train,
she took a lightning bolt
from her gingham apron
and handed it to me.

'This is a perihelion -
a facet of the mirror
that witnessed the
beginning of time,'
she explained.

We watched the sun
sketch psychotic poems
across a brilliantine canvas.

'There will be other trains,'
I told her.

The Tear Collector

The first time you saw me cry
was in the Italian restaurant
in Tunbridge Wells,
not the one
owned by the man
with the aggressive speech impediment
who bullied your brother at school,
the other one.
You plucked the tears
from my cheeks with a pair of
entomologist's tweezers,
as if they were rare Amazonian spiders
and placed them into
an album of
individually labelled
green plastic sleeves.

'This is the third,'
you said,
as you held the pustule of liquid
up to the light.
'It is a remnant
from the night
your father died,
when the Rabbi tried to take your hand
and you pulled it away.'

'This is the seventeenth,'
you said
and waved the tweezers
under my nose.
'It is the colour of betrayal
and will be shed in the future,
on the day you discover
that you have built
your life
on foundations
of cruelty and petulance.
It also shows you have a slight wheat intolerance.'

'This is the thirty sixth and last,'
you whispered
and placed what appeared to be
a shard of amethyst
into the palm of my hand.
'This is for today - for the first step of a thousand mile journey.
It is the same journey your father took
and his father before him
and it will lead you
back to me.'

You closed the album and hugged it to your chest
with proprietorial
ardour.
To you, this was only business.

Her 64th Boyfriend

I was her 64th boyfriend.
They came and went,
no more than
heads of corn in a thresher.
Terrified by their insignificance,
she began to kept count.

She lived on 45 West 139th Street
in Harlem
and slept with a loaded Webley
Mark IV revolver
under her pillow.
She shared her home
with a blind cat
called "Fury Goddess of Vengeance",
plagued by a highly contagious skin disorder
and with an albino rabbit
whose hind legs
had been replaced with
blue plastic wheels.

At 5.23am,
on our first morning together,
we listened to
"Chet Baker At the Forum"
as we lay in bed
and chain smoked Winston Blues
while, between rusted anecdotes,
we ate re heated churros
dipped in mucha-mucha spread.
Later, we knelt on her
lumpen mattress,
to stare through the frost monkeys
on the inside of her
bedroom window,
at the gang boys
on the broad walk below,
who strutted and preened,
naked as 50 watt fireflies.

When we fucked,
it was frenzied.
Our half filled cups of
jagged Ethiopian coffee
jousted on her bedside table
and afterwards, she held my face between fingers
twice her age
and I watched the
magellanic clouds
circle her eyes
in a parabola
of interstellar dust.

You Will Not Age Well

'You will not age well,' she told me.
It was 4.42am
on Valentine's Day 1988
and she was getting started.

I could not see her face
amongst the rust shavings
of early light
scattered over the concrete swathes of bedding,
but I knew it was there.

'I love you,' she said.
'But that has never been enough.'
As if love were a quantitative thing,
like a group of pensioners
huddled under
a rain blasted shelter
on the promenade
in Eastbourne,
or the green corduroy trousers
I wore to my
Bar Mitzvah.

I heard her pillow tumble and shatter onto the bedroom floor.
This was her move:
she touched my arm
and the temperature in the bedroom
plunged.

Her fingers ran down my side,
underneath my rib cage
and into my chest cavity,
where my heart used to be.
Her hand opened and closed in the
empty space
and for once,
for a few moments,
she had nothing to say.

Doubt Is My Mistress

Doubt is my mistress,
she teaches me to
trust my enemies and despise my friends;
she lays with me in bed at night,
squeezed under
the billowed fronds
where my wife cannot see her
scream into my face.

As my eyes begin to close,
I feel her fingers reach into my chest
and squeeze.

As the evenings close in,
I light tiny bonfires
to demarcate the homes of thieves.
Doubt has rented a flat with
Malevolence,
above the old jewellery shop
in the High Street.
Malevolence has a job
on the Co-op meat counter,
whilst Doubt weaves lies
into horses' tails and
works in a burger van
on Friday nights.

Tonight is Sunday and it is winter,
razor-white and brittle.
Doubt is unfurled
naked
on her tiny fold up bed;
she smokes a cigarillo
and distractedly sips a Chivas
from a green paper cup.
The ice rain wriggles
fractured rats' tails
down her bedroom window pane.

'I once knew Innocence,'
she tells me,
her nail-varnished toes
worm their way
up my thigh.
'That was before she moved to Felixstrasse 7 and became a whore.'

She reaches over me
to the ash tray behind my head;
our faces are close
and I can see the
lightning bolts
arc across her corneas.

She places her head
against my chest
and once again,
I can feel her jagged hands
close around my heart.

Tangerine Static

'I am not fucking around,'
she said,
her hair a cascade of melted sangria and burnt umber
across her pixelated eyes.

Butterfly kisses of frost
pocked the bedroom walls,
the single lightbulb ululated,
she stubbed and fizzed
and fumbled her doobie
into the paint stained mug of Thunderbird,
unfurled her arms into my jumper
and delivered another
hyperbolic sigh.

'We haven't left this room
for three days,' I said.
'And we can't until you give me a definitive answer,' she said,
as she took a gollop of VSOP
from the bottle and
gripping the tone arm between her toes,
she dropped the stylus
onto "Kimono My House"
by Sparks.

'I think it might be over,'
I said honestly.
'Honestly?' she asked.
'Then what is going to happen to me?'
She pointed a
peanut buttered fingernail at her chest.
'You?' I asked.
'Puta idiota, yes me.'
I shuffled along the bed, to the corner
where she had crawled
and folded her into my
cowardly embrace.
Her hair smelt of tangerine static,
her arms still fox cave moist warm
from the shower.

Our tears were fused positrons
on the lead edge
of a solar flare
that cavorted
with savage luminosity,
until the moment
of mutual annihilation.

The Duplicity Of Witches

For my 35th birthday,
we lay in the shed at the bottom of the garden
of our two by two,
 amongst a cornucopia
of rusting skeletons.
You wore your bridal veil
and a Pollyanna smile,
your squeeze-rinse hands
trembled covertly
in time, in time.

For the second anniversary
of our forty third kiss,
I was Otto Preminger
on the set of Bonjour Tristesse
and you were Jean Seberg.
We climbed the stairs
through the dovecote hatch,
our bodies planished
by a thousand wingtips,
hearts perseverated
with decrepitude,
as a single thorn of diffracted sunlight
illuminated
the predation of time.

On the night we fled from
perdition,
we abandoned our possessions
in the motel on the outskirts
of Cassiopeia,
our faces disordered
by entropy and fog rattle rain.
I realised we always
ran towards chaos
and this fingertip search
for the remnants of joy,
after our catastrophic collision,
had become
both our beginning
and our end.

On The Night When You Threw And I Ducked

On the day that I left Watford,
removal van crammed,
front door ajar,
my keys on the kitchen table,
beside the dent
from the frying pan,
on the night when you threw and I ducked,
I saw the hallway
we had festooned for Christmas and birthdays for 12 years
for the first time:
the stain where the plumbers we would never use again
had burst a bathroom pipe
and water poured down
on to the wallpaper we had no will to replace,
the well trodden trail
up the stairs
to the bedroom where you had once seduced me
and later where I would plummet
every night
into a well of fear so limitless
that I became madness
and that chamber my Bedlam,
the radiator that exploded
on the day our tears
shattered around our feet,
the promises our eyes gave each other
in the half remembered photographs on the wall.
You stood there
in the hallway,
a thousand miles away,
waiting for me to leave,
or not to leave, as I had not left before
and I stepped backwards
and forever
out into eternity.
For you, it was betrayal,
for me, freedom;
it was all the same.

Humbled By Darkness

I returned home on Christmas Eve
to find the house,
punctuated by a thousand
astral semicolons
when I left,
had been humbled
by darkness.
I reached for the light switch,
but there was only your hand
and your embrace.
It was the gateway to a garden
where every living thing
has perished
from insouciance.

'When we were first together,'
you told me,
your eyes as dangerous as feral dogs,
'you would kiss me in the morning
before you left for work
and then,
one day,
you stopped.
It authored
a divide
between us
so wide
that it could never be bridged,
but I knew that, if I
gave it a name,
it would own us.
So I called it Nothing
and that became
its name.'

You took my face in your hands
and led me to the reflections
in the ink stained hallway mirror.
I recognised you,
but no one else.

War

You bombarded me with platitudes
until my bunker shook,
until my nose was filled with
mustard gas and lexicography.

Your precious moral turpitude
scored a direct hit
that peppered me with shrapnel
and genteel verbosity.

You shouted, 'Dive'
and delivered a type 93 torpedo
and a list of competitively priced estate agents.

Take your semi automatic rifle
and
your Clinique makeup remover,
your grenade launcher and your
Mac superfine blusher,
your stab vest and the red silk dress that no longer
fits you.

Everything that was here
is now there:
behind enemy lines,
between the border patrol
and the gastropub
that used to be a wine bar,
that used to be a gastropub.

You said, 'Fire in the hole' and
'I love you but not
that kind of love.'
Perhaps it was the kind that only soldiers
understand,
when a war ends.

There is no battlefield.
There is no victory
or defeat.
But I do
surrender.

Four Reasons To Fear Love

First

I met her when I was
almost eighteen.
Her hair was spun
from the claws
of forgotten regrets
and her lips
tasted of
car park
drunken fumbles.

Years later,
on my wedding day,
I toyed with
the scar
left by her acrid laughter
on the back of my neck.
It was the shape of dishonesty
and often
bled.

Second

I was never more naked
than
on the evening
her parents returned home
early
from the Rayners Lane Odeon
to discover us on the carpet
in their bedroom,
our bodies smeared
with blue woad
and reticence.

I wore her mother's wedding dress.
Her father's face
was the crimson of
Oedipus's gore stained fingers,
a colour I have since discovered
is not available
in the Dulux Interiors match-pot range.

Third

When I was bisected
by a surgeon's cutlass
after my hernia operation,
she linked arms with me
in an axiomatic daisy chain
and we struggle-staggered
together
to the bathroom
every day
for a month.
Once I had recovered
fully,
she poisoned me
systematically
with the Lethal Furry mushroom
(Cortinarius orellanus)
she had personally sourced on a trip to the Ukraine.
How she loved a paradox.

Fourth

She abandoned me,
buried up to my neck
on the sea front
in Leamington Spa.

Her face was obscured
behind a puce yellow ski mask,
emblazoned with an
inverted crucifix,
she normally only wore
to funerals.

'This was love,' she said.
Tiny shards of hubris glittered in the corners of her opal shaped eyes.
'This is murder,' I replied.
She stroked my face with tenderness
and
with practiced grace,
she head-butted me.

'In the world I come from,'
she said.
'They are one and the same.'

Mars

'I am going to live on Mars,'
she told me,
schoolgirl shoe-scuffing at
the planished patina
of our marriage.

'I am to become a Cosmonaut, describing a languid proprioception
around earth
in a recalcitrant copper tube,
before being
boomeranged
out into the lacrimose
spacial void.

Through the ice bullets
and hellstones
we will sail,
beast crammed
cheek by jowl,
on a seven month
voyage
to the red planet.

On Mars, we will reside
in polyplastic huts,
at once bastard hot
and bitch cold,
suffering one brutal punch after another,
choking and straining and
grasping and starving,
on a glittering crimson amethyst
amongst the stars.'

'Is this about me
forgetting to empty
the dishwasher?'
I asked.

'No,' she replied.

'Forgetting to empty
the bin then?'

'Forgetting to empty the dog?'

'No,' she said,
juggling
fractals of anger
from side to side
across her monobrow.

'You had told me you planned to
move to Lyme Regis,' I said.

'Yes.
This is 33.9 million miles further,'
she said. 'I checked.'

'When you are
plunging through space,
what is to become of our love?' I asked.

'This isn't love,'
she replied.
'It is the shadow cast
by the explosive collision
of two disparate worlds.'

'Are you going to put that in the divorce petition?' I asked.

'I am leaving,' she said,
picking up a very small
suitcase and opening the
front door.

'That is a very small suitcase,'
I said.

'It is empty,' she replied.

'If you had moved to
Lyme Regis,
it would have been
easier
for you to have
come back to me,
to us,'
I said,
looking down at the dog
for corroboration.

Before the door closed,
she turned
and touched my hand -
a moment of
inter dimensional transition
frozen in
space and time.

'No, it wouldn't,'
she said.

'This is one of the most original books I have read in years. I love the author's style, and the humour throughout. This book deserves a much wider audience. I have recommended this to all the discerning readers I know!'
- John Brackenridge

Author's Profile

Laurie Avadis and Mark Donnegan founded a band (whose name must never be spoken) in 1980. By 1985, after signing a production deal, *The Last Postmen* were launched on an unsuspecting world. Radio airplay and headline gigs followed and TLP (as no one is calling them) have never disbanded. Laurie formed *The Nightingale Experience* with Steve Lewis in 2011. They have played the Festival Du Musique in Loire, Camden Live and in 2018 reached number 2 in the London electronic charts. They are still going strong and their music can be found on SoundCloud and ReverbNation.

Laurie held a major exhibition of his poetry and sketches in the Peggy Jay Gallery in Hampstead, with his sister Simone Bloom, for 10 days in September 2019. You can see his photography at laurieavadis on Instagram and he accepts photographic commissions.

His first novel 'Ex' a black comedy was published by Unbound in 2015 and distributed by Penguin and is still available for purchase on Amazon.

Laurie is a member of Viceroys Triathlon Club and is a very keen triathlete, regularly competing in races at sprint and Olympic distances.

He founded Avadis and Co solicitors in 1998 and continues to be a family court advocate for adults and children

He has written poems, lyrics and prose of some description since he was a teenager. Many of his early works have disappeared in love letters, on the back of placemats, on palms and fists.

Poems do not cascade from him - this has never been a conveyor belt, more a stuttering gazebo at once majestic and ramshackle. This collection contains his work from the last 10 years and tells an intensely personal story.

Like his novel 'Ex', this book was written with unbridled passion. Sometimes this manifests in humour, sometimes anger, but always raw honesty. If you read this and you recognise yourself, or someone you loved, then just know that whilst this may not be your truth, or their truth, it is Laurie Avadis's truth.

More titles available from Cerasus Poetry:

'painting for lemonade'
by sj howarth

'Last Night I Met John Adcock'
by Ewan Lawrie

'OUTBRANCHING'
by Scharlie Meeuws

'I dreamt I wrote another me'
by Alex Smith

'Waiting For Another Velvet Morning'
by Julia Macpherson

'Swim With Me In Deep Water'
by Penny Sharman

'According To The Dandelions'
by John Wilks

'Crown Of Eggshell'
by Rachel Deering

All books are available on Amazon
or on our website:
www.cerasuspoetry.com

Drop us a line at
cerasuspoetry@gmail.com
and request a free ebook
containing extracts from our first 6 titles

Printed in Poland
by Amazon Fulfillment
Poland Sp. z o.o., Wrocław